A SON OF MOTHER INDIA ANSWERS

A SON OF MOTHER INDIA ANSWERS

DHAN GOPAL MUKERJI

GYAN

Published by

GYAN

Gyan Publishing House
5, Ansari Road
Daryaganj, New Delhi-110002
Phone: 011-47034999, 9811692060
E-mail: books@gyanbooks.com

Distribution Network
gyanbooks.com
India, USA, Canada, UK, Australia

ISBN: 978-93-6920-573-8 (PB)

First Published, 1928

2nd Impression 2025

Printed at: Gyan Press, Delhi.

A SON OF MOTHER INDIA ANSWERS
Author: DHAN GOPAL MUKERJI

A SON
OF
MOTHER INDIA
ANSWERS

A SON OF MOTHER INDIA ANSWERS

BY

DHAN GOPAL MUKERJI

Author of "My Brother's Face," "Caste and Outcast," etc.

E. P. DUTTON & COMPANY · NEW YORK

M C M X X V I I I

TO

MR. & MRS. SAMUEL FELS

PREFACE

AFTER I had written my answer to Miss Mayo it occurred to me that my book would need a preface which should contain the following: "The writer who essays to criticize such a book as 'Mother India' labors under an important disadvantage which should be noted. Denials and doubts are cold. The original author, having a positive thesis to advance, makes affirmations, and may illustrate them with every available sort of instance or supposed instance; he or she can be concrete and picturesque. But the critic's position, especially in such an instance as the present one, does not allow of pictorial qualities.

"In order to give added life and vim, two obvious courses are open. One is to say *Tu quoque!* There are horrible products of Western civilisation which might be thrown in the teeth of the traducer of the East—the abject slums of this industrial nation, the appalling white slavery of that. And so on. The other course would be to lighten up one's reply with invective—and invective, shrewdly used, can be very telling.

"But it has seemed to me that to use either weapon against Miss Mayo could give but a passing and unreal advantage. And, besides, I think it is not my way. If I have tried to be temperate (though it has not always been easy) in this little book, and if I have avoided the temptation to build up a competing scene, it is because, first, two uses of a wrong method do not create a right one; and, besides, the weaknesses of Miss Mayo's case surely need only to be calmly indicated in order to make them plain; and then, second, because it ought not to be the way of India to reply in kind. Ancient and immemorial faith in gentleness, such as our seers and prophets have preached and practised, should make us as sweetly reasonable, as ready to admit the possible worthiness even of an unjust chastiser's motives, as hurt feelings and profaned sanctities can allow."

D. G. M.

A SON
OF
MOTHER INDIA
ANSWERS

Man animates all he can and sees only that which he animates.—Emerson.

CHAPTER ONE

I WAS very reluctant to read Miss Mayo's "Mother India," because I almost never read books about my country written by tourists. They, to my mind, never touch the depths and enjoy exploiting the surfaces. Were it not for the uproar that "Mother India" has caused in England and India, I would have avoided reading even reviews of it, but friend after friend, mostly Americans, sent me copies of it insisting that I give an opinion on Miss Mayo's indictment of my country.

I have searched in vain in many important English journals for a Hindu's review of Miss Mayo's book. I have failed to find an Indian's criticism of it in any significant American publication. In my own country, with the exception of Mahatma Gandhi's weekly, to no magazine or newspaper owned and edited by Hindus was a copy of the book sent for review, unless this has been done very recently.

The reviews that I read in the English journals were so extreme that I could hardly take the book seriously. At last I heard of the refusal of the London "Times" to print a protest signed by many Indians of the Moderate Party.

When, after giving the book a favorable review, the "Times" refused to publish the criticism of these Indians, who have a stake in their country, I was impelled to read what my countrymen had said. Indian journals such as "The Indian Social Reformer," printed the letter. It was written by Zoroastrians, Hindus, and Mohammedans who said:

> Our attention has been drawn to the recent publication entitled "Mother India" by the American tourist Miss Katherine Mayo, who paid a visit to India, during the cold weather of 1925-26. . . . We concede that like all other cold weather tourists Miss Mayo is entitled to form and express her own opinions. But when a foreigner who spends no more than a few months in our country, uses the material gleaned from hospital cases, culled from criminal trial reports, and de-

> duced from her own observations of isolated happenings and seeks to fortify herself with quotations divorced from their context and then proceeds on such slender basis to formulate a general indictment against the character and culture of a great country like India, possessed of an ancient civilization, and depicts an entire nation of 320 millions of people as physical degenerates, moral perverts and unabashed liars, it is time to enter an emphatic protest against the broadcast dissemination of these scandalous libels.

Those and other words of condemnation of "Mother India" are from statesmen, to name several, like Sir Tej Bahadur Sapru (Hindu), Sir Mohammad Rafique (Mohammedan) and Sir M. Bhownagree (Parsi). Even the High Commissioner of India did not hesitate to sign that protest. After reading the strictures passed on the book by those men I found it my duty as an Indian who speaks on Hindu culture to make a study of it in order to give my honest opinion to those Americans before whom I lecture.

I must say that my first reading of Miss

Mayo's work produced a sense of dismay in me. How can a book full of sharp criticisms bear the title and the dedication that it does? How can it have anything to do with such a word as Mother? In it not a single virtue of India is mentioned. If I understand the word Mother, which in our language is *Mata* or *Matri,* it symbolizes unending intimacy, tenderness, love, and respect. The significance of the word in English is the same. Suddenly a thing so intimate and close to one's life is slapped right on the title page of a book full of criticisms. What is one to make of it? But the American reader may ask, "Is not 'Mother India' a literal translation of *Bharatmata?*" It is. But we, her sons, when we use the phrase, do it with love, tenderness, appreciation, respect, and intimacy. Judged by the contents of her book Miss Mayo has been more technical than tender. There are not half a dozen pages of appreciation of *Bharatmata* in the whole book. That title "Mother India" is a misnomer. After I got through the title I had to meet the dedication. We hold that only he who appreciates and respects can dedicate anything to us. At least that is the way dedication sounds to one. Suddenly, page after page is dedicated to us like so many dagger thrusts. A very remarkable concept of dedication! The authoress herself admits at the end of her book that she has given us many wounds. No doubt she mitigates it by saying that those are the wounds inflicted by a friend. To that a Hindu would say: "If those are the wounds of a friend, what would an enemy inflict?" To my own thinking, Miss Mayo would have escaped the charge of shedding crocodile tears if she had attacked us with the audacity of an enemy.

But for the sake of the argument, conceding that she is our friend, let us consider the central theme of her book, which is a diagnosis of the disease that is killing India. Of course, she is not the first diagnostician from the West. Before her came many. Each one told us of the nature of our trouble. Of the Christian missionaries, the ablest diagnostician, Dubois, who, by the way, was paid a pension by the British, insists that India's ailments come from her religion. That is one diagnosis. And the remedy that would cure the malady is conversion of the Hindus to Christianity.

The second set of specialists that have looked at our troubles are the British imperial officials. Their diagnosis is that our sufferings arise from our inability to rule ourselves. What is the cure for that? Let the British rule both the Hindus and the Mohammedans and thus correct the disability that Nature herself put there.

The author of "Mother India" does not belong to those two classes of physicians, though she agrees with both of them on some points. She is modern and up to date. She is the eloquent discoverer of something tremendous. She has detected the root of India's trouble in sex. It is new and startling. Let us listen to her own words:

> The whole pyramid of the Indian's woes, material and spiritual—poverty, sickness, ignorance, political minority, melancholy, ineffectiveness, not forgetting that subconscious conviction of inferiority which he forever bares and advertises by his gnawing and imaginative alertness for social affronts—rests on a rock bottom physical base. This base is, simply, his manner of getting into the world and his sex-life thenceforward.
>
> The Indian girl, in common practice, looks for motherhood nine months after

reaching puberty—or anywhere between the ages of fourteen and eight. The latter age is extreme, although in some sections not exceptional; the former is well above the average.[1]

Yet we know that sixty per cent of the girls marry[2] after fourteen. In defense of her allegations that a Hindu girl attains motherhood at an age much nearer eight than fourteen Miss Mayo refers us to the Indian census report of 1921, which I have looked up. There I find no clear-cut assertion of age. On the contrary the report (Census of India 1921, Vol. 1, page 151, Chapter 7, says:

> It must be borne in mind, however, that the statistics of the married in India cannot be used without close analysis. Owing to the custom of infant and child marriage (no age specified) among Hindus and Jains, the figures contain a large number of unions which are little more than irrevocable betrothals. A Hindu girl-wife as a rule returns after the wedding ceremony to her parents' house and lives there

[1] "Mother India," page 22.
[2] See note of India Census, page 24.

until she reaches puberty, when another ceremony is performed and she goes to her husband and enters upon the real duties of wifehood. At the younger ages, therefore, the wives are not wives at all for practical purposes, though their future lives are committed.

And since 1892 the Indian Penal Code has made intercourse with a girl below twelve a criminal offense. That is quite different from Miss Mayo's definite statement that wives become mothers between the ages of eight and fourteen.

The difference between those two ceremonies, of betrothal and home-coming, I portrayed in "Caste and Outcast." They help to give the reader a sense of perspective in which to see things. Bearing that in mind, now we turn to the evidence of an English doctor, Miss M. I. Balfour, who resides in India. It stands to reason that she who has been practicing medicine there is much nearer the truth than Miss Mayo who merely travelled through the country. Dr. Balfour contradicts the figures given by Miss Mayo. The New York "Times" cable reads:

A woman doctor, Miss Balfour, practicing here writing to the "Times of India," combats the ages of motherhood given by Katherine Mayo in "Mother India."

Miss Mayo said the Indian girl commonly looks for motherhood between the ages of fourteen and eight, and that although eight was extreme, fourteen was well above the average age of motherhood. Miss Balfour records the cases of 304 Indian mothers who were delivered of their first babies in Bombay hospitals, and the average age was 18.7 years. Only three were aged fourteen, and they were the youngest.

Reports for the years 1922 to 1924 of the Madras Maternity Hospital, where 2,312 mothers were delivered of their first babies, show that the average age was 19.4. There were seven mothers aged thirteen and twenty-two aged fourteen. Miss Balfour also has reports of 2,964 cases in other parts of India, including the North, of which only ten cases were below fifteen years, and thirteen was the youngest age.

Miss Balfour, however, agrees that childbirth sometimes occurs too early in India and that legislation is badly needed.

The reader will notice that Miss Balfour speaks of southern India and also of the north. In the Allahabad "Leader" of October the fifteenth last, she says: "I think the figures I have given prove that the cases instanced by Miss Mayo do not in the least represent the common customs of the country."

The census report for all India is quite right about the two marriages. If strict adherence to facts were maintained in Miss Mayo's book she could have cited betrothal, the so-called first wedding, and the second, gauna, or consummation of the same, years later when the girl is passed puberty. Gauna is an obligatory religious custom. No wedded pair can come together without that ceremony held before their families and neighbors. Miss Mayo gives the following incident which startles me. She says that she came across a girl mother, at nine and a half, by Caesarian operation, of a boy weighing *one and three quarter pounds.*[1]

Granted that Miss Mayo did not know of the Indian Penal Code and did not inform the Police about that case, still one more thing remains to be proven: namely, that

[1] "Mother India," page 56.

this one personal experience of hers is not a criminal exception.

How dangerous it is to generalize about the Hindus of different sections of India will be clear to the reader from the following extract from Sir Denzil Ibbetson: "Wherever, in fact, marriage is the custom, the bride and bridegroom do not come together till a second ceremony called Muklawa has been performed, till when the bride lives as a virgin in her father's house. This second ceremony is separated from the actual wedding by an interval of three, five, seven, nine, or eleven years, and the girl's parents fix the time for it. Thus it often happens that the earlier in life marriage takes place, the later cohabitation begins." ("Leader," September 19, 1927.)

In the above, Sir Denzil is talking of the Punjab. Now, we turn to the United Provinces of Agra and Oudh. There, the census commissioner in his report for 1921 says, "Marriage among the Hindus means no more than irrevocable betrothal. The parties do not begin to live together immediately after the ceremony, but after the lapse of an indefinite period, generally of not less than one and not more than five years."

Similarly about Bengal, my own province, the first marriage, though it takes place before the bride has matured, the consummation of it is postponed until after puberty. In Bengal as well as in the joint provinces of Behar and Orissa, even the age of the first marriage has gone up in recent years. I must say fifty years ago when our social reformers such as Vidyasagar and Keshub Sen took up the cause of the girl-wives, things were probably bad in Bengal, Behar and Orissa. But thanks to the start given by them half a century ago the age of the girl-wives has been going up from year to year.

"It is apparent (page 159) from these figures that both in Bengal and in the two provinces together there has been a steady rise in the average age at which marriage takes place." (Census of India, 1921).[1]

[1] Census of India, 1921, Volume I, part 1, page 159.

	Number unmarried per mille males		*Number unmarried per mille females*	
	Aged	Aged	Aged	Aged
Year	10–15	15–20	5–10	10–15
1881	843	617	——	481
1921	879	687	907	601

Those figures show that (1) Nearly 70% of Indian males remain unmarried till they are out of 15–20 age group; (2) over 60% of Indian girls cross the age period 10–15 in unmarried state; (3) there has been a steady progress in the advance of the age of marriage since 1881.

Next I shall ask the reader to note that what Miss Mayo says about the debate in the Indian Legislature regarding raising the age of consent is just the reverse of what we know to be the fact. Because her information is the opposite of ours the reader must go into the proceedings of the Indian Legislature and analyze the votes that were cast in 1926. "Copious extracts," says Mr. P. Sapru in the 'Leader,' "have been given in the book ('Mother India') from the discussion on the Age of Consent Bill to show that Indian opinion is, generally speaking, opposed to any measure for protecting girl-wives. From reading the chapters one gathers the impression that the opposition to the measure came from Indian members only. *That a majority of the Hindu members were for raising the age of consent both within and outside the marital relationship would be clear to anyone who cares to go through the various debates on the Age of Consent Bill (now Act*[2]). The (British) Government's position was one of extreme caution. It was not even prepared to accept Sir Hari Singh Gour's amendment which would have raised the age of consent outside the marital

[2] Italics mine.

relationship to 15. An analysis of the voting on this amendment shows that a majority of the Hindu members voted for it and it was defeated by the (British) official votes. The position of the Government in regard to this amendment was thus stated by Mr. Tonkinson: "We are unable to accept any increase in the age outside of marital relationship above fourteen years." With the exception of Mr. Chalmers, all the unofficial Europeans (Britons), including Sir Willoughby Carey, Colonel Crawford, Sir Henry Stanyon, and the Rev. Dr. MacPhail voted against it. Hardly more satisfactory was the attitude of the Government towards the proposals which would have raised the age within the marital relationship to fourteen. The marriageable age of girls in recent years has gone up and this fact was emphasized by Dr. Datta in one of his speeches on the Age of Consent Bill. We are airily told, by 'Mother India,' however, that the Government of India has been exercising persuasive pressure towards progress and change; that it has to be cautious and that this caution is the more obligatory because of the tendency of the Indian public man to satisfy his sense of duty by the mere empty passing of a law.

But we must not forget that India is not the only country that finds it difficult to enforce laws. In any case I must request the reader to go into an analysis of the votes cast on the Age of Consent Bill of 1926 and decide for himself whether it was the Hindus or the (British) officials who defeated the raising of the age from that of twelve years, as sanctioned in 1892, to fourteen years as the majority of the Hindus wanted in 1926. And fourteen in the tropics would make a person as mature as seventeen in New York.

The above is corroborated by a European lady, Margaret E. Cousins, who is quoted in the Calcutta "Modern Review," November, 1927:

> I have lived in India for twelve years in intimate friendship with the women of India, with its students, and with its political and social reformers. My work along those lines was viewed so favorably that I was the first woman Honorary Magistrate in India. . . . The awakened women of India have for the past ten years, through their organizations, been asking the (British) Government to raise the Age of Consent; the Social Reform Con-

ferences have been doing the same since Raja Ram Mohun Roy's day.

Ten thousand women from one district alone have sent a petition to British Government to raise the Age of Consent. The representatives of over seven thousand more women who had assembled to discuss educational reform, also asked the Government to enact legislation asking marriage before sixteen years old for a girl a penal offense. All these facts Miss Mayo fails to note. Instead she descends to untruthful invention, when she says: "The Bill for raising the Age of Consent to fourteen was finally thrown out, buried under an avalanche of popular disapproval." There was not a meeting held all over India to express disapproval of the raising of the Age of Consent . . . If the British members of the assembly had supported the Bill, girls of fourteen would not now be legally approved mothers. We women definitely charge the British Government with delaying social reforms for which the people of the country are ripe.

[For further light on the same subject see "Modern Review," Nov., 1927. Also see Appendix IV.]

Apart from statistical figures, that can be disputed as we have shown, Miss Mayo places great reliance on the opinions of persons who are either dead or prefer to remain anonymous, which defeats all our efforts to cross-question them. Of the former group a missionary, the Abbé Dubois, is the one she quotes the most. It turns out that the Abbé, Christian priest thought he was, was given a pension by the British Government, ("Modern Review," Calcutta, Sept. and Oct., 1927) after he had finished his book of attacks on the Hindus and Hinduism. That is damaging enough. Besides, his evidence is as difficult to test as would be cross-examining a witness who does not appear in person in a law court. Dubois happens to be dead. He, after ambushing himself behind a grave, can afford to attack a whole race with impunity. Unlike him, there are other dead men who have said kind things about the Hindu. Somehow their names are not visible in "Mother India." Either their opinions do not lend themselves to Miss Mayo's thesis or their psychology is so different that they are of no use to her at the moment.

Another point to bear in mind about the Abbé is this: He was a missionary who wrote of the India of 1848. Miss Mayo quotes him without prominently mentioning that he was writing not today but three quarters of a century ago. He makes many sweeping assertions without giving adequate grounds. For instance, the scandalous charge he makes against barren women, and certain Brahmins in the Temple of Venkateswara. That sordid view we have to take on his own assertion. What did he know about the temple in whose inmost sanctuary he was not permitted to enter? No meat-eater has ever seen an interior where the holy of holies is kept. That did not prevent the Abbé from talking as if he were an eye-witness. He did not hesitate to traduce many heathen men and women. And does Miss Mayo want to imply that what he alleged against the Brahmins of one or two temples in 1848 could be said now in 1928? About this point of hers, *an English critic,* Wyndham Lewis in "Enemy," No. 2, has said: "Again there is the fact that the information taken from the account of the Abbé Dubois is not necessarily quoted in his words. It is mixed up with material from 'Young India,' Sept. 2, 1926, and that of other unspecified sources, and so recounted by the author as though part of one story, in result making the generalizations of the Abbé Dubois appear something that had happened yesterday."

Probably it will serve us better to bear in mind certain peculiarities about India. Our climate is mostly tropical. In such a latitude a plant grows as much in a week as it would in a month in *New England.* About human beings it can be safely said that a young girl of twelve in India is as old as a young woman of fifteen in America. As a parallel one sees marriages at an early age in the Mediterranean countries. In Calabria and Andalusia girls marry at an age much younger than in Northern Europe. Whatever custom we have are the results of our climate or of historical exigencies. Hence they are explicable to those who dig deeply for their causes. Our last significant peculiarity is that the Hindu religion is an indigenous thing. The religion of the Europeans and the Americans is of Eastern origin. It came from a soil other than their own. On the contrary Hinduism grew with the Hindu people on their own soil. In spite of their differences Christianity and Hinduism have one failing in common. Though their respective revelations do not sanction certain of their practices, yet the

Christians and Hindus persist in them. Nowhere do I find any support of wars and crusades in the words of Christ, yet Christians go to war with the approval and support of their clergy. In the Vedas and the Upanishads we find no sanction of seclusion of women (Purdah), yet the Hindus in many parts of India practice not only it, but also caste. Whatever the statistics of Indian marriages may be found to be, they are not based on the revealed words of God in the Indian Scriptures.

As a case in point, let me cite the following from "Mother India." In it the reader will see that even a keen-eyed observer may confuse our Bible with what it is not. "Little in the popular Hindu code suggests self-restraint in any direction," says our authoress on her own authority (page 27). Then without informing us about the nature of the code, whether written or unwritten, (Shastra or Deshachara) authoritative or not (Shruti or Smriti) she cites an Indian barrister who says "My father taught me wisely in my boyhood how to avoid infection." Next to that barrister whose character also we cannot judge because his name is not given, Miss Mayo quotes "a famous mystic" who indulges in sensual pleasures believing that "no question of right or wrong can be involved in any aspect of such matters." I can see that a barrister can remain a barrister after he indulges in sex irregularity. But no Eastern mystic can be honored as such if he goes even so far as to think of an impure act and let alone doing it, so strict is our standard for authentic mystics. For among our mystics we count such characters as Buddha, Jesus, who too was an eastern mystic, Chaitnya, Kabir, Nanak, and Rama Krishna. And I must add that Miss Mayo will do the Hindus and other races a real service if she will name the man in order to warn the world of such a base impostor. He is an insult to all religions.

Already I have referred to what Miss Mayo says about the age of motherhood of the Hindu girls, and the sex-life of the Hindu from the time he is born. About the latter she gives no authority save the force of her language. One of her unreliable yet most powerful pronouncements on sex is found on page 25.

> This, also, is a matter neither of rank nor of special ignorance. In fact, so far

are they from seeing good and evil as we see good and evil that the mother, high caste or low caste, will practice upon her own children—the girl 'to make her sleep well' the boy to 'make him manly' an abuse, which the boy, at least, is apt to continue daily for the rest of his life.

This last point should be noticed. Highest medical authority in widely scattered sections attests that every child brought under observation, for whatever reason, bears on its body the signs of this habit.

The above anonymous statement is all the foundation we have for a universal indictment of Hindu mothers, either of low or high caste. No hospital, no name of a doctor of any repute, not even statistics given. I had a mother. My sisters brought up boys and girls. My sister-in-law is a mother. My friends' wives are mothers. But not one of them indulges in such a horrible crime and vice. In any court of law, I would be ready to swear that all the Indian mothers that I have known never indulge in such a vile practice. "The highest medical Authority," who has not the courage to give his name in print, lied criminally to Miss Mayo when he made such a sinister charge against all the mothers of India. If he be a man, let him come forth with facts and figures. Now that the worst has been said the facts and figures should be given if any such can be produced.

In the entire book most of the serious charges are made by people who are dead, or, if living, their names are generally not given. Had their names been printed we could face them with the printed words. In cases where persons' names as well as their opinions are given, contradictions have been made, as we shall see later.

May I request Miss Mayo to print names and addresses? Any doctor or other authority bringing to light a case of perversion will be acclaimed as a benefactor. We need to know in order to be able to organize a vice-crusade. Our authoress owes it to her own sense of public decency to reveal to the world the exact sources of her knowledge. Otherwise we cannot be blamed for dismissing her general charges as untrustworthy.

Perhaps it will be interesting to learn how she places the persons whose opinions she reports without giving their names. Casually I open her book. My eyes fall on page 331, where the words of "trained American Observer" fill quite a paragraph. But, in vain I search for the name of her compatriot. On page 211 we are presented with the remarks "of one of the most eminent living Indians." Alas, we are not told his name. We cannot find out whether he is Gandhi, Srinivassa Sastri, The Nizam of Hyderabad, Lord Sinha, or an obscure person.

But to all the anonymous great, I prefer her own forceful words. They at least tell us which way the wind of her mind blows. Let us examine her generalization about the nationalism-bitten province of Bengal.

"Bengal," she says, "is the seat of bitterest political unrest—the producer of India's main crop of anarchists, bomb-throwers, and assassins. Bengal is also among the most sexually exaggerated regions of India and medical and police authorities in any country observe the link between that quality and queer criminal minds." Which police, and what medical authorities we are not told. I suppose according to that generalization about Nationalists, all of the Fascists, who in order to save their country go about with pistols, bombs, and castor oil, are suffering from excessive sex. In short, like modern literature modern nationalists are pornerastic. But let us extend pornocracy all over Bengal as our authoress does and see where it will lead us.

In Bengal were born such women as Sarojini Naidu and Taroo Dutt. At least one of them is an ornament of English literature. Bengal bore Rama Krishna, and his wife the Saint, Sarada Devi, also their disciple Vivekananda. Among Bengalis we count such noble social and spiritual reformers as Ram Mohun Roy and Debendranath Tagore. Many of the Indian scientists such as Roy, Sah, Dutt, Ghosh, Bose and Nilratan Sarkar come from Bengal. Tagore, one of the four authors of The British Empire to win the Nobel Prize for Literature, is a Bengali poet. Of the passionate and noble nationalists the Bengalis, Sarojini Naidu and C. R. Das are world-famous.

According to the "Indian Social Reformer" what Miss Mayo says against the Bengalis without any validity is this, "many little bookstalls where narrow-chested, anæmic, young Indian students, in native dress, brood over piles of fly-blown Russian pamphlets." The words "Russian pamphlets" bristle with fierce red possibilities. But there is no chance of such an occurrence, because according to the Post Office and Sea Customs Acts the police not only proscribe but confiscate any such literature. How can young men, no matter how anæmic, read in broad daylight piles of Russian pamphlets in places where not only the police but even a newcomer like our authoress can see them?

But there are things that a newcomer sees clearly, for instance, our system of caste. Even such an unfortunate subject as the untouchable outcasts of India we cannot leave without pointing out the programmes of constructive reform that are being carried out. I cannot give here the long history of the struggles and victory that the pariahs won at Vaikom. Nor can I give here the list of intercaste dinners and marriages that I witnessed when I was in India. That they are becoming frequent the perusal of the "Indian Social Reformer" week by week will convince anyone. During his recent trip through India and Ceylon, Gandhi was driven to conclude that the tyranny of caste is breaking down faster and faster. The results of the past five years' campaign have been so successful that the Mahatma and his followers are attacking the old tyranny with renewed energy. [Appendix II.]

In fairness to Miss Mayo I must set down here that she does not ascribe the conflict between Brahmins and the Pariahs to any sex-origin. However, that is one of the not numerous exceptions in her book. But here is another sweeping statement that demonstrates her conviction that the problem of India is derived from sex:

> From one end of the land to the other the average male Hindu of thirty years, provided he has means to command his pleasures, is an old man, and that from seven to eight of every ten such males between the ages of twenty-five and thirty are impotent.

Who told her that? How does she know? Where are her facts and figures? On whose authority, anonymous or otherwise, does she base her charge? We may be able to meet statistics with statistics. But how can any one fight convictions?

Another assertion, (page 25) made without any authority, is appalling:

> In many parts of the country, north and south, the little boy, his mind so prepared,

> is likely, if physically attractive, to be drafted for the satisfaction of grown men, or to be regularly attached to a temple, in the capacity of prostitute. Neither parent as a rule sees any harm in this, but is, rather, flattered that the son has been found pleasing.

Does Miss Mayo want us to believe that this is allowed by the children's guardians? She does not tell us the number of little boys who are victims, where, when, and how. In India the laws against this particular practice are as severe as elsewhere. We are not shown a single record of police court trials which might give us an inkling of its widespread prevalence. Here facts and figures are essentially necessary if the people of India are to be expected to combat the evil mentioned. Not only for the sake of her reputation as a reporter but for the purpose of eradicating the vice—if it exists!—from our midst we should be told of the exact number of cases and the places of their occurrence known to her. It is a moral necessity.

Of course my personal experiences are the reverse of Miss Mayo's. All the friends of my boyhood and I were taught Brahmacharya, purity of mind and body. That one must keep his mind, that mirror of God, and that Temple of the Deity, his body, pure and perfect is what an average child is taught. In our house we were four boys. Three of us are still living and we are willing to go before a board of inquiry and can say on oath that we and our friends never heard of the practice mentioned in "Mother India."

It can be safely asserted that not only does the soul and the culture of the country forbid this crime, but the Penal Code too is rigorously applied by the police against those abnormal persons who may commit it. Under such circumstances if our authoress has heard of numerous cases, as a humanitarian, she must give us the *names and addresses of her informants.* She should go to India once more and point out the exact plague spots. Otherwise there is no point in her making the statements that she does. Not only the Indian public but also the Police deserve to be helped. If such help be denied us then out of a sense of justice "Mother India" should exclude the horrible charges that it contains, in any further editions.

If the feeling that the book is a medley of mere opinions grows on its reader, he is not altogether to blame. Not only does Miss Mayo make sweeping statements on anonymous authority but she sets down hear-say reports of unpleasant nature which she admits she hesitates to believe. Some people told the authoress that young daughters of peasants cannot go out in the fields because they are afraid of being assaulted by the men working there. Miss Mayo "hesitated" to believe what she heard. ("Mother India," page 112). That allegation is contrary to my knowledge of four different provinces of India. In the face of my knowledge that all peasant women go about unmolested in the fields, I had to read her book over again. I find no chapter and verse there. She gives no statistics of trials in any police court where cases for assault in the rural districts were brought. Why did she not go to the British courts of Justice where the Police bring such cases? Instead of any court records we are informed that certain orientals as well as occidentals told her so. And she expects our credulity to devour what hers hesitated to swallow.

One of her inconsistencies is that though she believes the Hindus to be untruthful yet she quotes them whenever they happen to serve her purpose. Wherever those Hindus "hit hard in order to drive fast" the horses of Social Reform, she quotes them assuming that the hard hits are nothing but the truth. All reformers attack the hardest for they expect the best. In fact they believe and expect India to possess a "sky-scraping" spiritual greatness! She does not say anywhere in her work whether she knows Hindusthani well enough to converse with our common people. Nor does she avow that she gathered the impression that Hindus are liars by having long talks with English-speaking Indians. All that we have to go by is the opinion of an Englishman who has lived in India. This authority too remains anonymous in the book.

Let me quote against this anonymity, Judge Sleeman, who resided in India nearly a quarter of a century: "I have had before me hundreds of cases in which a man's property, liberty, or life has depended upon his telling a lie, and he has refused to tell it."[1]

Since we are on the subject of the virtues that the Hindus may possess, it can do no harm if we catalogue several of them. Let us ask: Are Indians Moral?

[1] Dutt's "Civilization in Ancient India," page 159.

In December 1901 at a meeting of the East India Association, Sir Lepel Griffin, the President said:

> The Hindu creed is monotheistic and of very high ethical value: and when I look back on my life in India and the thousands of good friends I have left there among all classes of the native community, when I remember those honorable, industrious, orderly, law-abiding, sober, manly men, I look over England and wonder whether there is anything in Christianity which can give a higher ethical creed than that which is now professed by the large majority of the people of India. I do not see it in London Society; I do not see it in the slums of East End; I do not see it on the London Stock Exchange. I think the morality of India will compare very favorably with the morality of any country in Western Europe. ("Modern Review," Calcutta, Oct., 1927, page 423.)

To the question whether Indians have spirituality and intellect, Sir Michael Sadler, President of the Calcutta University Commission, answered in 1919, in his University town of Leeds:

One cannot walk through the streets of any centre of population in India without meeting face after face which is eloquent of thought, of fine feeling, and of insight into the profounder things of life. In a very true sense the people of India are nearer to the spiritual heart of things than we in England are. As for brain power, there is that in India which is comparable with the best in our country.

While we are talking of spirituality let me say here that what caused me the keenest disappointment in "Mother India" were the references to, and photographs of, holy men. Miss Mayo gives us pictures of wanderers and fakirs and then informs that they are really holy men.

Outside of Gandhi, who is a holy man, there is no mention of a Hindu whom his compatriots would call "hundred percent" holy. Nowhere do I find references to such men and women as Rama Tirtha, Shraddhananda, Turyananda, Omkar, Saradananda and Sarada Devi. She, the last named was probably the holiest of them all.

I am afraid Miss Mayo was taken in by Babajis, Mendicants, and Moosafeers, Wanderers. Any day I can take her to a Hindu or a Mohammadan holy man who is second to none in the whole world. I wonder why she did not seek out such a holy man as Puran Bhagat, and the Lama, whom Mr. Kipling, one of the keenest of English observers, describes in his well known "Kim." Why did she not photograph them?

Speaking of her photography, let me comment on one more thing. In her book, there is a picture of a Hindu woman and her child. The mother, in order to make the child sleep gives it opium, is the message of that photograph. Alas, Miss Mayo, who never hesitates to rake up everything, does not tell us that the raising and auctioning of opium is a monopoly of the Christian rulers of India. That poor woman could not procure one blessed dose of it, if the State (British) did not raise opium for commercial purposes. In spite of our protests, opium and alcohol are allowed to be sold in every part of India.

Another vice that "civilization" brought us is syphilis.[1] That curse we received after

[1] "Reference Handbook of Medical Sciences," page 77: "The years 1493–1500 marked the introduction of syphilis throughout Europe, Asia and the Far East, following the voyages of discovery."

See, also, Frederick Tice, M.D., in "Practice of Medicine," vol. III, page 442.

the West discovered the sea-route to the East. It is working its havoc in those places of India where modern western civilization holds its greatest sway. Distilleries, owned and maintained by Christian nations, through augmenting trade have spread the blight of alcoholism in the East. Our doctors are struggling heroically with the abominations created by syphilis. But that is not enough. We must be enabled to fight alcohol and opium. [See Appendix.]

About the prevalence of venereal diseases, "Mother India," takes us to a particular Indian hospital where Purdah ladies are treated. "Most of the work here is gynecological. Most of the women are very young. Almost all are venereally affected." The words "almost all" and "venereally affected" should be paid attention to. Does Miss Mayo mean that a majority of the upper class ladies of all India are tainted with such diseases? Or, does she mean in one particular hospital in one given locality "almost all" the cases show such a state of affairs? What about the women of the middle and lower classes? Do their cases also bear the same taint? I should like to know the exact number of cases in that one particular hospital so that I can compare them with those that we find in a similar place in New York. The four words "almost all venereally affected" pronounced by Miss Mayo or by an anonymous authority serve to confuse the reader's mind. It may drive him to conclude that even those Hindus who do not go to hospitals are sick, too.

The climax of charges is reached in the mention of fourteen cases of outrage committed on young girls below twelve in 1891. Mind you a dozen cases nearly forty years ago in a country containing about three hundred million people!

What I sought and still am searching for is the exact number of cases of that kind in 1926. Instead of vivid phrasing we ask for the number of those certified by doctors. But all that we get is the general affirmation that "this same petition of the women surgeons was once more brought forward as equally applicable after the lapse of years." That cannot be true, for as I have already mentioned, our penal code does not permit any sex-relation with a girl below twelve. Let me reiterate here that a girl passed twelve in tropical India is much older than a girl of the same age in New England. If the police forces and the Indian Penal Code can be trusted, then the conditions prevailing in 1891 do not apply to the India of today. "Mother India" could be a trustworthy book if it would give clinical data. For ambiguous charges hurt the book itself.

At this point the reader may ask for the reason of our authoress for making the absurd sweeping statements with which her book is filled. Most of her statements go to fortify the idea that the Hindus belong to a degenerate race. Be that as it may, if we look at such books as "The Broken Road" and "A Passage to India," and the play "The Green Goddess," we will see in them that all Indians whether Hindu or Moslem suffer from the assumption of the Westerner that the Orientals are sex-addicts. In one of those three typical works, the author has the genius and the art to point out that the so-called viciousness of the Indian is an assumption not based on adequate facts. Mr. Forster deserves the gratitude of all impartial humanity for having pricked that bubble of misconception in his "Passage to India." Only a real artist and a man of genius could have done the task with such subtle clarity. When we come to mere men of talent such as Archer and the author of "The Broken Road" we can at once see that they did not hesitate to exploit the unreasoned prejudice of the man in the street. They were more interested in writing their works than in exploding undesirable myths.

So far, fortunately, the wretched assumption has resided in the house of fiction. Now suddenly Miss Mayo puts it in a serious work of travel. Her impossible thesis, let me repeat, is that "the whole pyramid of India's woes, material and spiritual . . . rests upon a rock-bottom physical base. This base is, simply, his [the Indian's] manner of getting into the world and *his sex-life thence forward*" (Italics mine). What until now has been a half-serious assumption of the average person of the West suddenly is offered as a scientific reality on which we are expected to pin all the Indian problems. There is no reason why this hypothesis should not be put forward. After all, many scientists work for one hypothesis or another.

But to my mind the untenable thesis of "Mother India" is hard to maintain with accurate scientific data, from the psychopathic wards of different hospitals, for the reason that India has not an adequate number of hospitals, nor more than a dozen psychopathic wards to supply sufficient evidence. In a country of three hundred million and more human beings where modern medical science has not yet established numerous clinics—for instance India has no Rockefeller Institute—an hypothesis like Miss Mayo's can be supported only by slender facts and stout generalisations. It is a pity all Hindusthan has not yet developed a very elaborate system of hospitals and clinics where a scientific thesis can be tested out in the light of carefully assembled facts. Our lack of scientific apparatus leaves India at the mercy of Miss Mayo's wild generalisations. Since we shall speak of all this again when we appraise the constructive elements of "Mother India," it will be better for us in the meantime to learn what Gandhi and others think of the book.

NOTE.—But it will do us no harm to recapitulate that the average age of motherhood in India is 18.3 years. Mr. Alden Clark establishes this fact beyond any dispute in his essay appearing in the "Atlantic Monthly" of February, 1928. "Even in cases of child marriage, first motherhood comes at an age when it can generally be normal." He further says, about the Census Appendix VII, on which Miss Mayo relies so strongly, that "cohabitation begins with puberty." The Punjab investigator also discovered that "in the majority of cases the first child is born in the third year of effective marriage."

Therefore, the reader can safely infer that in "common practice" the large majority of Hindu girls do not become mothers during the age mentioned by Miss Mayo,

CHAPTER II

I HAVE already intimated that some of the persons whom Miss Mayo quotes and whose names she prints have recently contradicted the statements attributed to them by her. Among them we count Miss Bose, who is at the helm of the Victoria College of Lahore, Gandhi and Tagore.

Before we come to their contradictions certain gossip-mongers who have been whispering that the Christian missionaries in India are supporting the charges in "Mother India" should be disposed of. I am glad to say that many idle rumours have been set at rest by the following from the Western missionaries:

Poona, October 17th, 1927

A statement with regard to Miss Mayo's "Mother India" signed by Rev. Dr. N. Macnicol and Mr. P. O. Philip, secretaries, and Miss A. B. Van Doren, Hon. Officer, has been issued to the press in the name of the Executive of the National Christian Council of India, Burma and Ceylon, the only dissentient member being Bishop J. W. Robinson, who does not find that he can assent to its terms.

The Lord Bishop of Calcutta and Metropolitan of India is the Chairman, and Dr. S. D. Datta, Vice Chairman of the Council, and the Executive Committee includes Rev. Chitambar, Bishop of Dornakal, Rev. J. F. Edwards, Dr. C. R. Greenfield, Bishop of Madras, Rev. J. Mackenzie, Rai Bahadur, A. C. Mukerjee, Messrs. K. T. Paul and B. L. Rallia and Rev. H. C. Velte.

The prominence that has been given to Miss Mayo's book, "Mother India," in Great Britain and America and the deductions which are being drawn from it, render it, in our opinion and in the opinion of many of our friends, necessary for the National Christian Council to issue some statement about it. Miss Mayo denies that the book was inspired by any third party, whether political or missionary. Nevertheless, it has been stated that the book was promoted in the interests of missionary propaganda. If these suggestions were true, we desire to repudiate emphatically any such missionary propaganda; but we wish to say publicly that so far as we have been able to discover, it is absolutely unfounded.

It has never been denied either by Indians or by foreign missionaries that grave social evils exist in India and it is a matter of common knowledge that strenuous and organized efforts are being made by groups of Indian reformers to get rid of them. Yet we, representing a body of men and women, who are in close touch with the people and are conversant with their everyday life, *unhesitatingly assert that the picture of India which emerges from Miss Mayo's book is untrue to the facts and unjust to the people of India.*"[1]

—*Associated Press*

That proves conclusively that the National Christian Council do not stand behind "Mother India."

After the Council's denunciation of the book I should like to give the opinions of two of the many individual Christians who do not support Miss Mayo.

[1] **Italics mine.**

Mr. Cavert says in the Federal Council Bulletin:

> When the distinguished British Quaker, Lucy Gardner, returned from several weeks in America she wrote that a visit to a foreign land ought always to be regarded as a sacrament—a reverent entering into the inner life of a people and a self-identifications with them in their deepest aspirations.
>
> We suggest to Miss Katherine Mayo that she ponder these wise words before she writes another book like "Mother India."
>
> We have read her much-discussed book with a sinking heart. And not so much because of the appalling conditions in India, so vividly portrayed, as because of the painful failure of Miss Mayo to approach her subject in that spirit of sympathetic appreciation which alone gives one any moral right to criticize the evil in others. At the moment, in connection with this review, we are not so much troubled by the distressing picture of India as by an American's own self-revelation of attitudes which gravely disqualify her from being

an interpreter of the life of another racial group than her own.

After reading the four hundred and forty pages of Miss Mayo's volume we cannot recall a single paragraph which records a pleasant or appreciative thing about the Indian people. She deliberately paints a black picture, excluding all rays of sunlight, making no effort to understand anything of the better side of Hindu life or thought. That seems to us a much more damning comment about the author's fitness for her task than about the country of India.

Having ourselves spent less than a year in India we do not undertake to pass judgment upon the detailed accuracy of Miss Mayo's observations. That most of the facts which she reports are substantially correct may indeed be true. We do, however, urge the need for caution in accepting her easy generalizations uncritically. Such thoroughly reliable journals as the *Review* of the National Christian Council of India, the *Indian Witness* and the *Indian Social Reformer*, we note, are taking sharp exception to not a few of her statements. Her glib remark, to take a single illustration, that "the Indian girl, in common practice, looks for motherhood nine months after reaching puberty, or anywhere between the ages of fourteen and eight," seems badly damaged by records of the maternity hospitals in Bombay and Madras. No one can doubt that most Indian girls marry too early, but, according to the statements of Miss Margaret Balfour, M.D., who has been collecting data for maternity and infant welfare work, several hundred cases of Hindu mothers delivered of their first babies in Bombay hospitals showed an average age of 18.7 years. In Madras, in the years 1922–1924, with 2,312 cases, the average age was 19.4 years.

What we chiefly object to, however, is not inaccuracy or bluntness in relating the worst conditions in India. The conditions would, in large part, be readily admitted by the most thoughtful Indian leaders, especially those who have been touched by the influence of Christ. *Young India,* for example, and *The Indian Social Reformer* —to mention but two editorial voices—have long been urging their own people to face grim evils in the Indian social structure. What we vigorously object to is the wilful refusal (or perhaps it is a temperamental inability) to bring into the picture many other things without which no one can hope to make a true appraisal. Even if all her statements about India be facts, it is certain that they do not constitute *the truth* about India.

Even if Miss Mayo has given us a statement wholly correct, by no stretch of the imagination can it be called *"Mother India."* There are realities there which Miss Mayo's racial myopia makes it impossible for her to see. No one who has really known, through personal acquaintance or through their printed word, Indians like Gandhi, Tagore, Professor Bose, S. K. Datta, K. T. Paul or K. Natarajan, could ever write so hopelessly one-sided and unbalanced a book as Miss Mayo has given us.

We should like to suggest to Miss Mayo that she write one more book, this time about America. We outline for her the following chapter headings:

"The Only Land Where Lynchings Occur"

The Land of Marital Scandal—One Divorce to Every Seven Marriages"

"The Land of the Crime Wave—Armored Motors Necessary to Transport Payrolls"

"The Land of Industrial Strife—Incessant Strikes and Lockouts"

"Child Laborers—A Million and a Half No Older Than Thirteen—in the Richest Land in the World"

All the *facts* in this new book might be impeccably correct, but would it be a picture of *America?*

We earnestly hope that whatever else may be thought of Miss Mayo's book—whether in India or in the United States—it will not for a moment be interpreted as reflecting the attitude of Christian missions. If we understand at all the missionaries in India (and it has been our good fortune to know several scores) the spirit of this book is the antithesis of theirs. Compare, for example, D. J. Fleming's "Building with India" or Stanley Jones' "Christ on the Indian Road" with "Mother India." They know all the evils of India even more fully than Miss Mayo, but they see what she fails to see—noble aspirations with which to sympathize and great qualities of soul to be admired and enlarged. Most of all, they do what the negative critic always fails to do—they associated themselves, in a spirit of sacrificial service, with all the best strivings and the best aspirations of the Indian people, confident that they and we together may build a better India, a better America, a better world.

To the preceding should be added the following letter from E. Stanley Jones, who, I am told, wrote that charming book "Christ on the Indian Road":

Bareilly, India.
November 28, 1927.

Miss Marie Butts,
Geneva.

Dear Miss Butts,

Thank you for your letter of the 11th of October regarding Miss Mayo's book. I entirely agree with you in regard to the damaging character of this book. A group of Americans residing in India including myself are just now sending out a signed statement protesting against the book. I hope this would be sufficient.

I will be in America in May and hope there to do what I can to counterbalance the effect of this exaggerated statement of the evils of Indian life.

I am glad for your concern regarding this deep injustice to India.

With greetings and best wishes,

Yours sincerely,

E. STANLEY JONES.

As regards statements of facts themselves and not "the author's generalisations" the "Leader" quotes Dr. Jones' opinion that they, the strict facts, can not be easily disproved. While conceding that he says, "I feel the book to be very unfair to say the least. . . . There is another India . . . But the India that I know is not there. And that India I love and respect and honour."

Since we cannot cross-examine those Indians and others who remain anonymous in the book we should turn now to the three Indians already mentioned, of whom we can ask questions. Let us see if they agree with our authoress. It is better that we should learn from them whether the statements attributed to them are well-founded. First of all comes the poet Tagore. Miss Mayo apparently did not interview him. But she tore out of context a passage from an essay of his and used it to prove that Tagore, too, believed in child-marriage. Now the truth of the matter is that the poet never champions child-marriage. He is speaking of early marriage. And anyone who has the remotest knowledge of Tagore's activities as a passionate social reformer and of his co-educational University can say that Miss Mayo is wrong. To associate Tagore with child-marriage is as fantastic as saying that Miss Jane Addams believes in Negro lynching.

I think it is easy to verify beliefs attributed to specific individuals. Anytime we feel that Miss Mayo has made a mistake we can ask the person named. If the reader would read "Forward" of Oct. 29th, "The Modern Review" of September and October last, and "The Indian Witness" he will find a long and detailed denial by Miss Bose of Lahore, of the opinions ascribed to her by our authoress. Of course it must be borne in mind that when a person is interviewing so many people one is bound to make errors. My belief is that those errors are not confined to the reported utterances of some of the persons named, but they also spread through the statements of many an anonymity. Even Gandhi, that soul of humility and forbearance, feels that witnesses who accuse India and do not offer themselves for cross-examination are difficult to believe. They, I feel strongly, embarrass their own testimony more than they know. Nothing is easier for them than to attack a whole continent from behind the veil of their anonymity. Here instead of speaking for Gandhi I shall let him speak in person.

> On the lips of the good, vice becomes virtue,
>
> And even virtue appears as vice in the mouth of the evil minded: this need not surprise us.
>
> For, do not the mighty clouds drink the salt waters of the ocean and return it as sweet refreshing rain,
>
> And does not the cobra, drinking sweet milk, belch it forth as the deadliest poison?
>
> The book is cleverly and powerfully

written. The carefully chosen quotations give it the appearance of a truthful book. But the impression it leaves on my mind is, that it is the report of a drain inspector sent out with the one purpose of opening and examining the drains of the country to be reported upon, or to give a graphic description of the stench exuded by the opened drains. If Miss Mayo had confessed that she had gone to India merely to open out and examine the drains of India, there would perhaps be little to complain about her compilation. But she says in effect with a certain amount of triumph, "The drains are India." True, in the concluding chapter there is a caution. But her caution is cleverly made to enforce her sweeping condemnation. I feel that no one who has any knowledge of India can possibly accept her terrible accusations against the thought and the life of the people of this unhappy country.

The authoress says she was dissatisfied with the literature she read about India, and so she came to India "to see what a volunteer unsubsidized, uncommitted and unattached, could observe of common things in daily human life."

After having read the book with great attention, I regret to say that I find it difficult to accept this claim. Unsubsidized she may be. Uncommitted and unattached she certainly fails to show herself in any page. We in India are accustomed to interested publications patronized,—"patronized" is accepted as an elegant synonym for "subsidized,"—by the Government. We have become used to understanding from pre-British days, that the art (perfected by the British) of government includes the harnessing of the secret services of men learned, and reported to be honest and honourable for shadowing suspects and for writing up the virtues of the Government of the day as if the certificate had come from disinterested quarters. I hope that Miss Mayo will not take offence if she comes under the shadow of such suspicion. It may be some consolation to her to know that even some of the best English friends of India have been so suspected.

But ruling out of consideration the suspicion, it remains to be seen why she has written this untruthful book. It is doubly untruthful. It is untruthful in that she condemns a whole nation or in her words "the peoples of India" (she will not have us as one nation) practically without any reservation as to their sanitation, morals, religion, etc. It is also untruthful because she claims for the British Government merits which cannot be sustained and which many an honest British officer would blush to see the Government credited with.

If she is not subsidized, Miss Mayo is an avowed Indophobe and Anglophil refusing to see anything good about Indians and anything bad about the British and their rule.

She does not give one an elevated idea of Western standard of judgment. Though she represents a class of sensational writers in the West, it is a class that, I flatter myself with the belief, is on the wane. There is a growing body of Americans who hate anything sensational, smart or crooked. But the pity of it is that there are still thousands in the West who delight in "shilling shockers." Nor are all the authoress's quotations or isolated facts truthfully stated. I propose to pick up those I have personal knowledge of. The book bristles with quotations torn from their contexts and with extracts which have been authoritatively challenged.

The authoress has violated all sense of propriety by associating the Poet's (Tagore) name with child-marriage. The Poet has indeed referred to early marriage as not an undesirable institution. But there is a world of difference between child-marriage and early marriage. If she had taken the trouble of making the acquaintance of the free and freedom-loving girls and women of Shantiniketan, she would have known the Poet's meaning of early marriage. (See appendix.)

She has done me the honour of quoting me frequently in support of her argument. Any person who collects extracts from a reformer's diary, tears them from their context and proceeds to condemn, on the strength of these, the people in whose midst the reformer has worked, would get no hearing from sane and unbiased readers or hearers. But in her hurry to see everything Indian in a bad light, she has not only taken liberty with my writings, but she has not thought it necessary even to verify through me certain things ascribed by her or others to me. In fact she has combined in her own person what we understand in India the judicial and the executive officer. She is both the prosecutor and the judge. She has described the visit to me, and informed her readers that there are always with me two "secretaries" who write down every word I say. I know that this is not a wilful perversion of facts. Nevertheless the statement is not true. I beg to inform her, that I have no one near me who has been appointed or who is expected to write down every word that I say. I have by me a co-worker called Mahadev Desai who is striving to out-Boswell Boswell and does, whenever he is near me, take down whatever he considers to be wisdom dropping from my lips. I can't repel his advances, even if I would, for the relationship between us is, like the Hindu marriage, indissoluble. But the real crime committed against me is described by her pages 387–88. She ascribes to the poet "a fervent declaration that Ayurvedic science surpasses anything that the West can offer." (She has this time no quotation to back her statement.) Then she quotes my opinion that hospitals are institutions for propagating sin, and then distorts out of all recognition a sacred incident, honourable to the British surgeons and I hope, to myself. I must ask the reader to excuse me for giving the full quotation from the book:

> "As he happened to be in the prison at the time, a British surgeon of the Indian Medical Service came straightway to see him. 'Mr. Gandhi,' said the surgeon, as the incident was then reported, 'I am sorry to tell you that you have appendicitis. If you were my patient I should operate at once. But you will probably prefer to call in your Ayurvedic physician.'
>
> "Mr. Gandhi proved otherwise minded.
>
> " 'I should prefer not to operate,' pursued the surgeon, 'because in case the outcome should be unfortunate, all your friends will lay it as a charge of malicious intent against us whose duty is to care for you.'
>
> " 'If you will only consent to operate,' pleaded Mr. Gandhi, 'I will call in my friends now, and explain to them that you do so at my request.'

> "So Mr. Gandhi wilfully went to an 'institution for propagating sin,' was operated upon by one of the 'worst of all,' an officer of the Indian Medical Service and was attentively nursed "through convalescence by an English Sister whom he is understood to have thought after all rather a 'useful sort of person.' "

This is a travesty of truth. I shall confine myself to correcting only what is libellous and not the other inaccuracies. There was no question here of calling in any Ayurvedic physician. Col. Maddock who performed the operation had the right, if he had so chosen, to perform the operation without a reference to me, and even in spite of me. But he and Surgeon-General Hooton showed a delicate consideration to me, and asked me whether I would wait for my own doctors who were known to them and who were also trained in the Western medical and surgical science. I would not be behind-hand in returning their courtesy and consideration, and I immediately told them that they could perform the operation without waiting for my doctors to whom they had telegraphed, and that I would gladly give them a note for their protection in the event of the operation miscarrying. I endeavoured to show that I had no distrust either in their ability or their good faith. It was to me a happy opportunity of demonstrating my personal good-will.

So far as my opinion about hospitals and the like is concerned, it stands, in spite of my having subjected myself and my wards to treatment more than once by physicians and surgeons, Indian and European, trained in the Western school of medicine. Similarly I use motor cars and railways, whilst holding to my condemnation of them as strongly as ever. I hold the body itself to be an evil and an impediment in my progress. But I see no inconsistency in my making use of it while it lasts, and trying in the best manner I know to use it for its own destruction. This is a sample of distortion of which I have a personal knowledge.

But the book is brimful of descriptions of incidents of which an average Indian, at any rate, has no knowledge. Thus she describes an ovation said to have been given to the Prince of Wales, of which Indian India has no knowledge, but which could not possibly escape it if it had happened. A crowd is reported to have fought its way to the Prince's car somewhere in Bombay. "The police," says Miss Mayo, "tried vainly to form a hedge around the car moving at a crawl unprotected now through a solid mass of shouting humanity which won through to the railway station at last." Then at the railway station, while there were three minutes for the train to steam out, the Prince is reported by Miss Mayo to have ordered the barriers to be dropped and the "mobs" to be let in. The authoress then proceeds, "Like the sweep of a river in floods, the interminable multitude rolled in, and shouted and laughed and wept, and when the train started, ran alongside the Royal carriage till they could run no more." All this is supposed to have happened in 1921 on the evening of Nov. 22nd, whilst the dying embers of the riots were still hot. There is much of this kind of stuff in this romantic chapter, which is headed "Behold a light."

The nineteenth chapter is a collection of

authorities in praise of the achievements of the Britich Government, almost every one of which has been repeatedly challenged both by English and Indian writers of unimpeachable integrity. The seventeenth chapter is written to show that we are a "world-menace." If as a result of Miss Mayo's effort the League of Nations is moved to declare India a segregated country unfit for exploitation, I have no doubt both the West and the East would be the gainers. We may then have our internecine wars. Hindus may be eaten up, as she threatens, by the hordes from the North-West and Central Asia,—that were a position infinitely superior to one of ever-growing emasculation. Even as electrocution is a humaner method of killing than the torturous method of roasting alive, so would a sudden overwhelming swoop from Central Asia upon the unresisting, insanitary, superstitious and sexuality-ridden Hindus, as Miss Mayo describes us to be, be a humane deliverance from the living and ignominious death which we are going through at the present moment. Unfortunately, however, such is not Miss Mayo's goal. Her case is to perpetuate white domination in India on the plea of India's unfitness to rule herself.

The picturesque statements that this clever authoress puts into the mouths of the various characters read like so many pages from a sensational novel in which no regard has to be paid to truth. Many of her statements seem to me to be utterly unworthy of belief and do not put the men and women to whom they are ascribed in a favourable light. Take for instance this statement put in the mouth of a prince:

> " 'Our treaties are with the Crown of England,' one of them said to me, with incisive calm. 'The princes of India made no treaty with a Government that included Bengali *babus*. We shall never deal with this new lot of Jacks-in-office. While Britain stays, Britain will send us English gentlemen to speak for the King Emperor, and all will be as it should be between friends. If Britain leaves, we, the princes will know how to straighten out India, even as princes should.' " Page 316.

However fallen Indian princes may be, I should want unimpeachable evidence before I could believe that there can be in India a prince so degraded as to make such a statement. Needless to say the authoress does not give the name of the prince.

A still more scandalous statement occurs on page 314 and reads as follows:

> " 'His Highness does not believe,' said the Dewan, 'that Britain is going to leave India. But still, under this new regime in England, they may be so ill-advised. So His Highness is getting his troops in shape, accumulating munitions and coining silver. And if the English do go, three months afterward, not a rupee or a virgin will be left in all Bengal.' "

The reader is kept in darkness as to the name of His Highness or of the enlightened Dewan. [According to the capital (Calcutta) this unfounded bit of gossip is over forty years old. D.G.M.]

There are many statements which Miss Mayo puts into the mouths of Englishmen and Englishwomen living in India. All I can say with reference to these statements is that if some of them were really made by the authors, they are unworthy of the trust reposed in them and they have done an injustice to their wards or patients as well as to the race to which they belong. I should be sorry indeed to think that there are many Englishmen and Englishwomen who say one thing to their Indian friends and another to their Western confidants. Those Englishmen and Englishwomen who may chance to read the sweepings gathered together by Miss Mayo with her muck-rake will recognise the statements I have in mind. In seeking to see an India degraded Miss Mayo has unconsciously degraded the characters whom she has used as her instruments for proving her facts which she boasts cannot be 'disproved or shaken.' I hope I have given sufficient *prima facie* proof in this article to show that many of her facts stand disproved even in isolation. Put together they give a wholly false picture.

But why am I writing this article? Not for the Indian readers but for the many American and English readers who read

Young India from week to week with sympathy and attention. I warn them against believing this book. *I do not remember having given the message Miss Mayo imputes to me. The only one present who took any notes at all has no recollection of the message imputed to me.* But I do know what message I give every American who comes to see me: "Do not believe newspapers and the catchy literature you get in America. But if you want to know anything about India, go to India as students, study India for yourself. If you cannot go, make a study of all that is written about India for her and against her and then form your own conclusions. The ordinary literature you get is either exaggerated vilification of India or exaggerated praise." I warn Americans and Englishmen against copying Miss Mayo. She came not with an open mind as she claims, but with her preconceived notions and prejudices which she betrays on every page, not excluding even the introductory chapter in which she recites the claim. She came to India not to see things with her own eyes, but to gather material three fourths of which she could as well have gathered in America.

That a book like Miss Mayo's can command a large circulation furnishes a sad commentary on Western literature and culture.

I am writing this article also in the hope, be it ever so distant, that Miss Mayo herself may relent and repent of having done, I hope unconsciously, atrocious injustice to an ancient people and equally atrocious injustice to the Americans by having exploited her undoubted ability to prejudice without warrant their minds against India. The irony of it all is that she has inscribed this book "To the peoples of India." She has certainly not written it as a reformer, and out of love. If I am mistaken in my estimate let her come back to India. Let her subject herself to cross-examination, and if her statements escape unhurt through the fire of cross-examination, let her live in our midst and reform our lives. So much for Miss Mayo and her readers.

I must now come to the other side of the picture. Whilst I consider the book to be unfit to be placed before Americans and Englishmen (for it can do no good to them) it is a book that every Indian can read with some degree of profit. We may repudiate the charge as it has been framed by her, but we may not repudiate the substance underlying the many allegations she has made. It is a good thing to see ourselves as others see us. We need not even examine the motive with which the book is written. A cautious reformer may make some use of it.

There are statements in it which demand investigation. For instance she says that the Vaishnava mark has an obscene meaning. I am a born Vaishnavite. I have perfect recollection of my visits to Vaishnava temples. Mine were orthodox people. I used to have the mark myself as a child, but neither I nor anyone else in our family ever knew that this harmless and rather elegant-looking mark had any obscene significance at all. I asked a party of Vaishnavites in Madras where this article is being written. They knew nothing about the alleged obscene significance. I do not therefore suggest that it never had such significance. But I do suggest that millions are unaware of the obscenity alleged to be behind it. It has remained for our Western visitors to acquaint us with the obscenity of many practices which we have hitherto innocently indulged in. It was in a missionary book that I first learnt that Shivalingam had any obscene significance at all, and even now when I see a Shivalingam neither the shape nor the association in which I see it suggests any obscenity. It was again in a missionary book that I learnt that the temples in Orissa were disfigured with obscene statues. When I went to Puri it was not without an effort that I was able to see those things. But I do know that the thousands who flock to the temple know nothing about the obscenity surrounding these figures. The people are unprepared and the figures do not obtrude themselves upon your gaze.

["Young India," Sept. 15, 1927.]

Nowhere in Mother India does its author give any facsimile of letters of approval from Gandhi. From the above quotations it seems clear that Gandhi never spoke the words that Miss Mayo puts into his mouth. If she has any letters from Gandhi she ought to print them.

CHAPTER THREE

ANYONE who has read the book more than once will be convinced that what hurt Miss Mayo's feelings most in India was the suffering of (1) women, (2) children, and (3) animals. That she was genuinely stirred by whatever suffering she witnessed is beyond question. And I believe that if her entire book could be reduced to what she saw and not what she was told, it would make a telling story of dirt, disease and death among women, men and children and those brothers of man—the dumb beasts. I personally think that meat-eating and ill-treatment of the animals are not the least of the sins for which Heaven will judge mankind. The sooner meat for diet and cruelty to animals are abolished the better the earth will be as a habitable place. The Hindus should give up every form of pain that they inflict on animals. And the non-Hindu ought to take to pure vegetarianism.[1]

I am afraid I have let my sympathy for

[1] About good treatment of Indian animals, see Alden Clark's paper. Feb. "Atlantic Monthly," 1928.

the brute carry me far afield. But that proves only too well that I agree with Miss Mayo about the poor suffering animals, as I share her sympathy for those Hindus whose numerous problems are unforgetable.

But what I do disagree with is her method of writing. She does not seem to realize that her book, to be effective, should appeal to the two races—the Hindu and the Anglo-Saxon. Though the latter is more or less convinced by "Mother India," yet the former remains utterly offended by the book. I am afraid that he is right if its many offensive generalizations keep him from reading it, and since it is of paramount importance that he should learn about his own woe as well as that of his beasts of burden, I sincerely request our authoress to sacrifice all the offensive and unreliable sweeping statements from her work and reduce it within such desirable limit as the strict facts of her observation would permit. If she does so then she will be read all over India, which will help the numerous Hindu social reformers in their arduous task of altering their society to square with the teachings of their scriptures. That India sees the need of social alterations is evident not only from the reformers' passionate utterances on that subject quoted by Miss Mayo, but also by what they have done in the past and what they are doing now. Her citations from Gandhi and others prove that because they desire to reform their society the Hindus have been attacking their own orthodoxy mercilessly. The force of their phrasing, the enthusiasm with which they are working and the results that they have already achieved are conclusive proof that old India is marching on a new road. Here Miss Mayo can yet do us some service. I believe she has that wish in mind. Though the manner in which she has written "Mother India" clouds that wish, yet one can believe that she really desires to serve those who suffer most in this world—the women and the children. This help she can render more effectively if she will only write so that she does not offend the Indians. If we eliminate from her book all the chapters that contain hasty generalizations, we shall compress "Mother India down to that irreducible minimum of personal experience, which no one will be able to gainsay. In fine the new edition of her book will be invincible if it deals with cruelty against animals and meat-eating, girls in child-bed, babies dying in large numbers, innumerable widows still remaining unmarried, and the caste-ridden pariahs. Of course, there is nothing original in citing those facts. No traveller seeing India in one winter can do more. A few glimpses of the obvious are all that any tourist can get in a few months. A few well established facts written in her compelling style will pierce into those recesses of the Hindu sensibility whence they cannot be dislodged. The kindness of heart that "Mother India" betrays in some paragraphs is genuine and strong, and it ought to be made serviceable to the suffering souls of men and beasts. I can already see with my mind's eye what such an edition of her book will do for her in India. It will make friends for her. She will be received with open arms into all the organizations for social reform. She will be acclaimed by the Arya Samaja, Brahmo Samaj, Seva Sadan, Rama Krishna Mission, Parthana Samaj, the All India Hindu Mahasava, and numerous other groups of social reformers.

The only thing that may stand in the way of my suggestion being put into effect is that Miss Mayo may refuse to eliminate the absurdities in her book which to my mind are numerous. They only help to swell the bulk of her book. Were it not a work of such wide range charged with errors, it might have been invulnerable. A smaller book could not have made as many mistakes as this one does. How can anyone travelling through a country without any great knowledge of its classical language and modern dialects write without mistakes on so many subjects as Education, History, Government, Politics, Sociology, and the Prince of Wales? It is humanly impossible. To such an impossible task if we add the central thesis of "Mother India" that sex is at the bottom of India's trouble, we can at once foresee the book's many blemishes. The stupendousness of the task is obvious.

After granting her assumption that she is unprejudiced and fair-minded we have still to find out whether we agree that the purpose for which she wrote the book as it stands is accomplished. That purpose, I take it, was two-fold: namely, (1) to maintain her thesis and (2) to urge a speedy amelioration of the condition of the Indian people. In order to test the soundness of her thesis about the sex-life of the Hindu we must seek the opinions of sex-experts and other specialists for more light on the subject. If they agree that the same trouble that underlies the unrest of the Modern West is eating up India, Indians need but rejoice. For that makes us as modern as the rest of the world. Nowadays a single touch of sex makes the whole world kin.

The study of sexuality in India is in its infancy. Nothing reliable, appertaining to the whole country, has as yet been published. Since we cannot have the opinion of any experts may we not be allowed to suspend judgment? I believe Miss Mayo's data do not warrant a sound inference. I, for one, am not yet convinced.

Assuming that the Anglo-American public is totally satisfied and agrees with Miss Mayo that India must clean her house, we have still to convince the public most concerned in this —the Hindus. The failure of her book lies in its having misrepresented the sons and daughters of Hindusthan. Not only men but also women have denounced it as untrue to the facts. For that reason I invite Miss Mayo to bring out a very short and new edition of the book packed with strict facts and ready clinical notes. In short, I am willing to offer myself to assist her to re-write the book. If it is done it will win all the Indian social reformers over to her side. Without further delay I set forth to outline the new edition.

We shall begin by giving credit to the Indians both Hindu and Moslem for the virtues that they possess. We shall praise them for their loyalty to Great Britain during the last war. We shall go even so far as to praise Gandhi for suspending the practice of his personal philosophy of non-violence during the period of the great conflict. We shall make mention of his contribution along with that of the princes and the common people to the morale and the physical efficiency of the Indian army. They did superb work wherever they were sent.

Having blessed the Indians for not stabbing England in the back at a very critical hour we shall give them credit for the virtue that they possess most next to loyalty: namely, gratitude. We shall show from the writings of Lord Roberts, Younghusband, and Lord Ronaldshay, and the diaries of many officials and numerous letters written by Englishmen and women, what a prominent part the sense of gratitude plays in the life of an Indian.

After that we shall praise him for his sense of duty, which he maintains in the most trying circumstances. Anyone who has read "Gunga Din," and "Kim" can testify how dutiful an Indian can be. Untold Hindus consider "duty heavier than a mountain and life lighter than a feather." And, of course, as a corollary to those virtues Indians must possess some truthfulness, humility, and generosity.

Having disposed of their virtues we shall give them due credit for their art and literature. As for their philosophy and mysticism we shall become "trumpet-tongued" in praise of both. We shall not hesitate to say with the western philosopher, "The Upanishads have been the solace of my life, let them be the solace of my death." I think our appreciation of his excellence has made the Hindu very receptive by now. Having won our way into his heart we can safely broach to him the question of (1) his excessive otherworldliness which is the source of all of his troubles, such as, (2) caste, (3) child-widows, (4) high rate of infant mortality, and (5) the seclusion of women known as Purdah.

It is not easy to find out the cause of our preference for other worldliness, and the Via Mystica. Instead of getting lost in the unfathomable abyss of research into the origin of the Hindus' devotion to mysticism we shall inform him that though God likes man to choose the better part, the way of Mary, it will be better for the Hindu race to take up the way of Martha for a while. If the Indians want to be respected by the self-governing nations of the world they should give up the Via Mystica and set their feet firmly on the path of Modern Science. I think, this idea presented with extreme graciousness and abundant humor, without invectives, will not fail to convince all India. Once the Hindus see eye to eye with Miss Mayo it will be easy for her to pursuade them and the British government to pass a law making excessive concentration on religion on the part of any individual a real crime. Here the reader may grow skeptical of the complete success of such a measure, nay, he may go further, and tell us of the strange set-backs that the Eighteenth Amendment has received here and there in the United States. But God-intoxication in Hindusthan like alcoholic intoxication can not be dealt with mercifully. I am speaking from a knowledge of my own people. If they are to abandon listening to the Son of God, like Mary, they will have to be dealt with similarly. And if we are backed by sufficient number of important Hindus we should, at any event, do our least as did the followers of Volstead in America.

The next thing that India should be told is that the relation of man and woman should be based on hygiene and eugenics; physiology should displace metaphysics. We shall appeal to the men in the name of the love and respect that they invariably feel for their women. Since the space at our disposal will not permit us to quote passages from the Brihadaranyaka Upanishad and other documents of the remote past that testify to the reverence and tenderness that Hindus have felt for their wives and mothers, we shall quote English witnesses of the past hundred years. Let us just cite two witnesses who will serve our purpose admirably.

In 1813 at the time of the renewal of the Charter of the East India Company Sir Thomas Munroe[1] was asked if Hindu wives were not the slaves of their husbands, Munroe replied "They have as much influence in their families, as I imagine, the women have in this country! . . . If . . . a treatment of

[1] Sir Thomas Munroe, a then very important official of the British East India Company's government.

the female sex full of confidence, respect and delicacy, be among the civilized people, then the Hindus are not inferior to the nations of Europe; and if civilization is to become an article of trade between the two countries, I am convinced that this country (England) will gain by the imported cargo."

About a hundred years later Flora Annie Steele [1] who lived many years in India writes: "To a Hindu man or woman marriage is a solemn religious duty. It is an absolutely inviolable sacrament, and divorce is unknown, the underlying theory being that before God the male and the female form together the perfect human being. Therefore, neither can worship apart from the other. Before such a belief as this, it is idle to talk about the woman's position being degraded. . . . Once married, a Hindu almost invariably becomes a perfect prey to his women folk, at any rate for some years. It is astonishing to what lengths the woman's influence may go." ("India," page 67.)

After the Hindu men have received credit for being tender and respectful to their women, Miss Mayo could demand of them

[1] Flora Annie Steele is the author of "Prince of Dreamers" and many other books on India.

two most fundamental reforms. She could say: If you really are so kind and noble, then give absolute equality to all of your sisters, mothers and wives. Make seclusion of women a crime, punishable by law. Allow women to choose their husbands. Nay, more than that, from now on make divorce as free and easy as in America and France. That reform, I hope, will put the relation of the sexes on a scientific basis throughout India.

Once those points are settled we shall find the question of the high death-rate of infants an easy one to tackle. All the Indians will join us in our crusade against it. Still, if there be some recalcitrant fellows, we should depict for them those few details and vivid personal experiences which Miss Mayo could take to court and swear are all true.

They are, as we all know, about the agonies of young mothers under the care of mid-wives. Our authoress and the European doctors are deeply distressed by what they have witnessed. Naturally it makes them indignant. Before rewriting her book, Miss Mayo must call upon thousands of Indian doctors. She could say to them: "Now we appeal to you who are working to alleviate the sufferings of your people!" After all, the majority of the medical men in India are Indians. We should go to the medical schools and colleges that are run at the taxpayer's expense, not to mention those institutions endowed by the Indian people. With our sympathy, we should sweep all India before us. We should not hesitate to note that the record of harm done by the mid-wives is rapidly diminishing, because the Indian doctors are growing in numbers. In India today the ablest doctors along with the ablest scientists and the best lawyers, are Indians. We should appeal to such Hindu doctors as Bidhan Roy and Nilratan Sirkar of Bengal, Dr. Subarao of Madras who is doing very advanced research work in Harvard, and last of all, to the important physicians from the other provinces of India. That would make us invincible; then it would be easy for us to break the mid-wives' hold on India. Of course we all know India is not the only country suffering from the ministrations of mid-wives.

Compare that appeal with what we have in "Mother India" at the present moment. In it in vain we search for the names of the talented Indian medical men and the progress that they have made in many directions toward ameliorating the sufferings of women and children. I am equally disappointed to find no reference to Indian "science institutes," their own endowments, run by their own scientists, some of whom are world famous.

Not only to our kind doctors but to Indians that are studying other branches of modern science we shall give the credit that they deserve. After all every world-famous man of science in India, is an Indian: For example, Rahman, Sah, P. C. Ray, Bose, Rasik Dutt, Ramanujan,[1] and Ghosh. And the scientists that they are training will do credit to the fair name of India in the near future.

Then we should do our utmost for the Hindu widows. For a while we must go very carefully. We must take special care to show how much has been already accomplished in that sphere. We must also reiterate what men and women under Rishi Debendra Tagore, Vidyasagar, Shraddhananda, Gandhi, Rananday and others have done against such deadening and time-worn customs and traditions as caste, suttee, and child-widowhood. We must also say that

[1] Ramanujan has been considered as remarkable as Euler or Jacobi.

owing to their efforts, India has made the advance that she has, and she should not rest on her oars. Then we should chide the Hindus for their slowness. We should satirise them for marrying girls below fourteen. We should be as merciless as an executioner, yet as tender as a mother

Before going any further Miss Mayo must seize the present opportunity and correct a great blemish in "Mother India"—its lack of perspective. For instance, nowhere in her book has she given a scientific statement of the processes of Indian history that explain the origin of the Caste System, and the genesis of the practice of Suttee (burning of the widows).

The reader should be permitted to know events that caused the existence of Suttee, of seclusion of women, of early marriage, and of enforced widowhood. I wish I could set forth here in great detail how, owing to a terrible exigency of history, widow-burning became a custom, and how later on the Hindu reformers led by Ram Mohun Roy abolished it. Since that will take too much time I am compelled to refer the reader to Dutt's "Indian History," Waley's "Pageant of India," page 178, and my "Caste and Outcast," where he will find the proper historical treatment of the origin and end of Suttee.

Having presented the causes of many of the Indian social customs and traditions with adequate and unbiased history Miss Mayo must not hesitate to praise the chief Indian reformer, Ram Mohun Roy, and his valiant fellow-workers without whose most persistent and consistent efforts the burning of the widows could not have been abolished nearly a century ago. (See "The Face of Silence.")

Though that custom, whose historical necessity had disappeared, was at that time done away with, the next logical step in social reform, the remarriage of the widows, was taken up by another man, Isvar Vidyasagar a few years after Ram Mohun's premature death. Vidyasagar like his predecessor was a Brahmin (priest) and the greatest Sanskrit scholar of his day. He showed from our scriptures that, as they give no sanction for Suttee, so they give no sanction for the enforced widowhood of women. He fought like a tiger for the re-inauguration of the custom of remarriage of widows—a custom that had been interrupted for nearly eight hundred years. He argued that since those harsh centuries and the exigency of our history had passed, it was natural and logical that widows should not only be permitted to live but also to remarry. After considerable work he succeeded. If Ram Mohun Roy was the morning star of Indian social reform, Isvar Vidyasagar was its risen sun. Had he not established, some forty years ago, the sanction given by our scriptures and theology that widows can remarry if they wish to do so, the Census Report of 1921 (page 161) would not say cheerfully:

> A considerable number of societies have been formed in different parts of India with the avowed object of encouraging the re-marriage of widows. One of the most successful of these has its headquarters in the Punjab where . . . there seems considerable scope for its enterprise, and it is conducted on the principles of the Sanatan Dharma as a Hindu institution. The Sabha (the Institution) claims to have caused the marriage of over 300 widows in 1921 and to have over 4,000 men registered in its books who desire to find widows to marry, and the latest report

> shows figures of marriages and applications in 1922 considerably larger than those quoted. Similar societies exist (in other provinces) Bengal, Bombay and South India, while the Arya Samaj and the other protestant religious (Hindu) sects are attempting to free the community from this obsolete restriction.

This shows that even the most delicate and difficult work of social reform is progressing well in India.

If I seem to presume to rewrite Miss Mayo's book for her, I beg the reader to note that I have done it to point out a golden opportunity that awaits her. She can yet enlist the Hindu people on her side by eliminating from the book all the errors and half-truths thus reducing it to a quarter of its present size. By concentrating on the five-fold root of India's troubles and by removing all offensive generalizations, she could make a book that would be fair to the Hindus and yet help to cure them of their present social ills.

She ought not to hesitate to sacrifice her rather difficult thesis in order to bear down the full weight of her sympathy for the

Hindu women and infants. If I were in her position I would not bother about sex being at the bottom of India's troubles. I would concentrate on the troubles that are provable. They are enough to keep one occupied.

I hope Miss Mayo will heed my counsel. I hope she will not be offended at my suggestions. On the contrary if she repeats the wild generalizations, edition after edition, she will have made an enemy of the Hindu race.

There is no doubt her book has done much harm. If the feelings and opinions of the Anglo-Saxon race are at all comprehensible to a Hindu then I must frankly say that "Mother India" has provided a lot of Anti-Hindu propaganda in England and America. In India the book has caused a great deal of Anti-Western agitation. The burden of all the oratory in many mass-meetings has been that "Mother India" proves that Westerners hate and despise us, therefore, away with Western imperialism. All the reports of the numerous meetings that I have read are charged with strong Anti-Western phrases and sentiments. They all accuse Miss Mayo of hitting a race that is down (conquered). Whether it is an accurate estimate or not, it seems to me that since the Amritsar Massacre there has not been anything that has created so much resentment against the British in particular and the West in general as the book under review. Can this be what Miss Mayo wished and intended? This raises the question whether its publication was worth the candle of race-hatred, that has been lighted. In the present state of world-affairs can we afford to speak and write so that instead of bridging, we widen the gulf between man and man? The answer to that question must come from the West since "Mother India" is the work of a Westerner, but India's own reply to Miss Mayo might well be in the words of my holy man in Benares:

"India needs love. The West has given her criticism these many years. . . . I am quite clear in what I am saying: love her and she will fulfill her destiny. . . .

"The world is suffering from judgment. Men talk philosophy to their brother writhing and bleeding on the ground, a spear planted in his heart. What the poor wounded man needs, they, the instructors of mankind, do not see; it is not the salt of judgment on his wound, but the strong hands of affection.

East and West are words that stab with criticism—drop thy words, like daggers by the roadside, and rush to thy Brother's rescue. . . . Bring out the Face of Compassion from within thy heart! Bathe the wounded body of man in the cleansing currents of thine inward peace."

THE END

APPENDICES

APPENDIX I

From "The Nation," January 4, 1928.

Rabindranath Tagore Says:

To the Editor of The Nation:

Sir: I came to know from the advertising columns of your paper that Miss Katherine Mayo's "Mother India" has been lauded by Arnold Bennett as "a shocking book, in the honorable sense." Unfortunately, for obvious reasons, there is a widely prevalent wish among the race that rules India to believe any detraction that may bring discredit upon India, and consequently the kind of shocks that Miss Mayo has manufactured offers them a delicious luxury of indignation. The numerous lies mixed with facts that have been dextrously manipulated by her for the production of these shocks are daily being exposed in our journals; but these will never reach the circle of readers which it is easy for Miss Mayo to delude. Along with other Eastern victims of lying propaganda we in India also must defenselessly suffer mud-besmearing from unscrupulous literature; for your writers have their machinery of publicity which is cruelly efficient for raining slanders from a region usually unapproachable by us, shattering our fair name in an appallingly wholesale manner.

I happen to be one of those whom the writer has specially honored with her attention and selected as a target for her midnight raid. Difficult though it is for me completely to defend myself from such a widespread range of mischief, I must try through your organ to reach the ears of at least some of my friends who are on the other side of the Atlantic and have, I hope, the chivalry to suspend their judgment about the veracity of these shocking statements, made by a casual tourist against a whole people, before lightly believing them to be honorable.

For my own defense, I shall use the following extract from a paper written by Mr. Natarajan, one of the most fearless critics of our social evils. He has incidentally dealt with the incriminating allegation against me deliberately concocted by Miss Mayo out of a few sentences from my contribution to Keyserling's "Book of Marriage"—cleverly burgling away their true meaning and shaping them into an utterly false testimony for her own nefarious purpose. Mr. Natarajan writes as follows:

> Tagore sets forth his own ideal of marriage in five long pages at the end of his paper (Keyserling, pp. 117 et seq.). "Let me," he says, "as an individual Indian, offer in conclusion my own personal contribution to the discussion of

the marriage question generally." He holds that the marriage system all over the world—and not only in India—from the earliest ages till now, is a barrier in the way of the true union of man and woman, which is possible only when "society shall be able to offer a large field for the creative work of women's special faculty without detracting the creative work in the home."

If Miss Katherine Mayo was not a purblind propagandist but an honest inquirer, and if she had not the patience to read Tagore's essay, she might have asked any one in Calcutta what the age of marriage of girls is in Tagore's own family. That she was determined to discredit the poet is evident.

Let me ask some of your readers to read my paper on Hindu marriage in Keyserling's book and challenge, in fairness to me, Miss Mayo to prove that it was my own opinion, as she asserts, that child marriage is "a flower of the sublimated spirit, a conquest over sexuality and materialism won by exalted intellect for the eugenic uplift of the race," implying "the conviction, simply, that Indian women must be securely bound and delivered before their womanhood is upon them, if they are to be kept in hand."

Let me in conclusion draw the attention of your readers to another amazing piece of false statement in which she introduces me, with a sneer, as a defender of the "Aruvedic" system of medicine against Western medical science. Let her prove this libel if she can.

There are other numerous witnesses who, like myself, if they find their access to the Western readers, will be able to place their complaints before them, informing them how their views have been misinterpreted, their words mutilated, and facts tortured into a deformity which is worse than untruth.

RABINDRANATH TAGORE

Santiniketan, India, November 9, 1927.

APPENDIX II

THAT Indian social reform is not a spasmodic thing can be gathered from the wide-spread attacks in different sections of the country on the privileges of the highest caste, the Brahmins. For instance, after steady non-violent resistance day after day for over eighteen months the Pariahs, untouchables, of Vykom won their rights. They have had redressed the grievances of centuries through the great sufferings of a dozen and a half months. It has affected not scores but hundreds of thousands of the oppressed classes of southern India. The hardships the passive resisters endured will become vivid to the reader if he reads "Young India" of April 24th, 1924. The victory at Vykom has set rolling the snow-ball of social revolution which in a decade more will become the avalanche of equality that will crush the monster of Caste under it.

There are many peaceful reforms that have improved the fate of thousands also. Take the way the large Baria community has ameliorated its own state. The reader will get a glimpse of their successful programme in the "Young India" of February 18, 1926. Since then further strides have been taken by the progressive Barias in every direction. The same steady progress has been made by the

Chandras ("Young India" June 24, 1926). In the December 30th, 1926 issue of the same weekly the reader will find the extensive improvement that the so-called Wardha Untouchables have wrought. Not only that, they are not resting on their oars. They are carrying on so successfully that the so-called high caste is abandoning more and more of its ancient privileges in order to come to terms with them.

How the peaceful reformers work out their programme I described in my paper that appeared several years ago in the "Standard." There I dwelt on the far-reaching case of the Kaliparjans. These depressed (oppressed?) folks have shown how *Satyagraha* or self-purification lifts a downtrodden community. I shall not mention here the success that crowned the efforts of the many Satyagraha movements like the Tarakeswar of Bengal where ancient property rights of the Mohunt, the property-holding priest, were radically modified by the passive resisters of Bengal.

The Tarakeswar Satyagraha and others like it are not so astounding as the one the Siromani Gurudwara Prandhak carried out. The sufferings endured by the Sikhs, a most advanced section of the Hindus, from August, 1922 until as late as 1926 were colossal. The "Manchester Guardian" of October 9, 1922, "Modern Review," of September, October and November, 1922, and "Young India," of January 10, 1924 will convince the reader that in order to deprive their Mohunts of their property and preposterous self-conceded rights the people suffered hardships that are unbelievable. At last when they emerged victorious, throughout the Sikh Community in particular, and the Hindu world in general, a shock of joy and courage was felt.

The results obtained at Vykom or those won by the Sikhs of Siromani Gurudwara show that India has set moving a vast machine of social revolution. We are seeing only the beginnings of it. Instead of pessimism the hearts of the people are filled with authentic optimism. No American can appreciate how fast India's social changes are being wrought simply because he has no conception how slow we can be. I personally feel that India is like an elephant—she is moving forward inevitably. The following is the latest illustration that shows how Gandhi is winning for the outcast untouchables their long-denied birth-right.

Berhampur, Dec. 11, 1927.

The Patitapavan Mission of the "Reform & Service League" presented addresses to Mahatma Gandhi at Ichapur and Berhampur on 4th and 6th instant respectively. In reply Mahatmaji spoke highly in favour of temple entry of the so-called untouchables. He made settlement with the trustee of the Raghunath Temple and entered into it with the untouchables at the close of the meeting at Berhampur.

—"Calcutta Forward," Dec. 15, 1927.

APPENDIX III

The meeting of the far Eastern Association of Tropical Medicine this year in Calcutta has awakened a sudden interest in health conditions prevailing in India. In the course of a written address delivered at the Rotary Club, Col. D. J. Graham described India as 'one of the world reservoirs of infection and the main reservoir of infection for plague and cholera.' Deathrate in India, Dr. Graham further remarked, was twice that of England and Wales; infantile mortality rate was nearly two and a half times that of England and Wales and nearly four and a half times that of New Zealand. In his inaugural address before the Tropical Medicine Congress the Bengal Governor made a frantic attempt to save his Government from the dire implications of these hard facts. It is during British rule that cholera and plague first made their appearance in India, but no systematic efforts have ever been made to save the people from the inroads of these diseases.

—"Calcutta Forward," Dec. 8, 1927.

APPENDIX IV

All India Social Reform Conference has pressed upon the whole country as well as the British government the following resolution:

Resuming this morning, with Mr. K. Natarajan in the chair, the Social Conference adopted resolutions relating to marriage reform, the status of women and social inequalities based on sex. The Conference favoured raising of minimum marriageable age for boys and girls to 21 and 16 respectively, supported the legislation for marriage reform now on the anvil in Delhi and Bombay and strongly condemned the indignities forced on Hindu widows.

—"Forward," Dec. 29, 1927.

Mrs. Reddi, a leading Hindu feminist, adds further that though the country is ripe for reforms the government, though Christian, yet does not help them. —"Forward," Dec. 30, 1927.

Few of us women who have come to the forefront of public life raise our voice on behalf of our suffering sisters and ask for reforms. We have memoralised and petitioned to the Government to strengthen the hands of our champions in the councils and in the Assembly and we naturally expect a good and enlightened Government to respond readily to our call for help and even if they do not find their way to take initiative in such good, urgent, and much needed reform, at least to embrace the very first opportunity given to them when private members bring any bill or resolution to improve the women's lot in this country; but to our dismay and disappointment, what do we find? We all know what the Government's attitude was when Mr. Sarda's bill was introduced. Even at this stage, in spite of our meetings, in spite of our memorials and petitions, the Government member Hon. Crerar brought a dilatory motion to delay such a good and urgent legislation on the plea of religious neutrality, even after our Hindu leaders like our Lala Lajput Roy, Mr. Jayakar, Mr. S. Sreenivasa Iyengar and Mr. M. K. Acharya have repeatedly assured that Hindu religion does not sanction child marriages and even after they found that enlightened Hindu opinion was in favour of the bill, even after the native states like Mysore, Baroda and Bharatpur legislated to that effect.

Again in the demand for the Devadasi legislation the representatives of the council have been asking for legislation for the last half a century or so to abolish the custom of dedicating young girls or young women to the temples for purposes of prostitution because nowadays whatever the original object might have been, dedication of a girl to a temple signifies nothing but dedication to a life of vice and our revered late lamented countrymen, Sir T. Sadasiva Iver and P. R. Sundaram Iver, in their judgment at the Madras High Court have said that dedicating a girl means initiating her into the life of a prostitute and there is no text in our religion that sanctions such an immoral institution and again in the G. O. of Mysore it is explicitly stated that the Devadasi institution has been done away within the Muzrai temples because of the immoral and vicious lives led by these women.

In 1912 and 1913 three bills were brought by Menakji Dadhabai, Mudholkar and Madge to suppress this evil. In 1924 Dr. Gour's resolution to abolish dedication in the temples had been voted upon unanimously by the Assembly. The 1924 amendment in the penal code having failed to stop the evil why is the delay on the part of the Government to put down once for all with an effective legislation the most heinous crime on earth? Mysore has tackled this Devadasi problem most wisely even as early as 1909. Cannot the enlightened British Government follow in the foot-steps of the progressive Native States even if they do not want to offend the orthodox feelings?

The other day what was the reply of the Government to the Hon. V. Ramadoss Pantulu's resolution to end the Devadasi system? Even to-day after 150 years of their stay with us, our Government seems to doubt the fact that the dedication of a girl amounts to her employment as a prostitute. Have we not given sufficient proof already by the vote of our councils? I may also point out to them once more that a resolution recommending to the Government to put down that pernicious practice with a firm hand has been unanimously voted upon by the Madras Council at its last session. Again the Government advised the Hon. V. Ramadoss to "educate the public opinion and start vigilance associations in the Presidency to prosecute the culprits."

As for educating the public opinion, we have been doing it for the last 60 years and we have wide public support behind us. If people could be so easily educated in these matters as to take the law in their own hands, where is the necessity for any Government or Parliament? Then without the help of legislation we will have to wait till the Doomsday for getting rid of these social evils. Even we women have become discontent and have begun to grumble at the indifferent and unsympathetic attitude of our Government towards social legislation in general.